Windows 10

A complete Windows 10 guide and user manual for beginners!

Table of Contents

Introduction

You may be considering upgrading to Windows 10 or perhaps you already have it.

Either way, the majority of Windows 10 users don't realize how amazing this operating system can be and how many different features it has that will completely change the way you navigate the internet and interact with your PC.

From voice-activated digital assistants and multiple virtual desktops to apps that know what kind of device you're using, and apps compatible with Xbox One, Windows 10 has plenty of upgraded features and also some brand new tools too. It is, by far, Microsoft's best version of Windows to date.

However, it can be overwhelming reading through hundreds of pages in the Windows manual that, unless you're an IT professional, can seem like it's written in an alien language, not to mention a pretty dull read. That's why I wrote this book which explains the main key features of Windows 10, how to use them, and how to overcome many common issues.

In this book, all the jargon and computer-speak has been left to one side to give you a complete guide to using Windows 10 in plain English. In the first chapter, I will explain what Windows 10 is and how it differs from older versions (and how it's much better than Windows 8.1, Microsoft's most-complained about Windows version). The following chapters will look at the benefits of using Microsoft 10, what it's new and exclusive features are, and how you can use them and customize them for your personal preferences. It also includes a Frequently Asked Questions section in the final chapter where you should find the answers to all your doubts and issues regarding Windows 10.

Before we look at all it's incredible tools and features, let's move onto Chapter One and find out: what is Windows 10?

Chapter 1: What Is Windows 10?

This chapter will explain what Windows 10 is and what makes it different from all the other Windows versions.

There are a lot of different Windows versions and for those out of the technology loop, it's easy to feel lost in what's what and how everything works.

Windows 10 – sometimes abbreviated to Win10 or WinX – is the latest version of Microsoft Windows. You would be forgiven for thinking that before Windows 10 it was the Windows 9 version but in fact, it wasn't; Microsoft skipped the Windows 9 version and upgraded to Windows 10 straight from Windows 8.1. It was released at the end of July, 2016; yet despite it being around for a few years, it still baffles people and a lot of users don't know its full potential or features.

That's because Windows 10 is extremely powerful – it's Microsoft's most powerful operating system so far– and, as a result, the most complex out of the Windows versions to use. The user interface is actually highly logical though and once you get used to it, easy to navigate; however, most users barely scratch the surface and fail to use the great features that Windows 10 provides, such as a customized experience, multiple desktops, and a voice assistant. It's all easy to find and use; it's mostly just a case of knowing where to look and how to activate it.

Microsoft described Windows 10 as an operating system that functions as a service, and it will continue to receive updates and tweaks throughout the course of its lifetime to improve its functionality and to add new features.

If you're used to the functions on Windows 8.1, here are some of the key differences between them:

• The full-screen 'modern' apps of Windows 8 which were touch-friendly and sometimes known as the 'Metro' or 'Modern' design, were often considered annoying by many users – at least, Microsoft received a high volume of complaints about them. If you're not sure what this means, this applies when you're using Windows on a tablet or 'smart' device. In Windows 10 these full-screen apps are optional so if the tablet is docked into the keyboard base, you can will see the usual desktop and once you take it off, you can then switch to the touch-friendly option you'll recognize from Windows 8.

• The start menu is also different. In addition to the apps, a lot of people didn't like the Windows 8's full screen Start menu. If you were one of those people, then you'll be pleased to know the Windows 10's start menu is back in the left side of the screen with that column of shortcuts and apps that we all recognize (and many of us love). What if you liked that full-screen Start menu in Windows 8? There is an option to customize it and even switch between the two modes using Continuum, a feature of Windows 10 that knows when you are using different devices and adapts the interface accordingly. We'll look at Continuum in more detail later. For now, it's worth knowing that there is also an option to completely get rid of the full screen Start menu too.

• Unlike Windows 8 or any other Windows versions for that matter, Windows 10 has a nifty function that allows you to arrange apps next to each other and make use of a quadrant screen that divides your display into up to four different apps. You can also have multiple virtual desktops to keep things organized, and a handy 'Task View' button on the taskbar that lets you see any files and windows you have open on your desktop, and to see all the desktops you are currently using.

• Internet Explorer is a little different on Windows 10. While Internet Explorer still exists, it has a new browser known as Microsoft Edge. It has all the features of a modern browser, which is something we'll look at in more details in a later chapter. There are some cool extra features as well, such as Microsoft's Virtual Assistant, Cortana, and the Web Note button where you can share notes from websites through OneNote or e-mail.

To use Windows 10, there are a couple of requirements. You need a 1GHz processor, 1GB of RAM at the bare minimum, and 16GB or more of hard drive space, so if you don't have Windows 10 already and are thinking of upgrading to it, check to see if your PC can support it.

So, to conclude, Windows 10 is the latest operating system of Microsoft and it comes with a whole bunch of incredible features that not enough users know about, which is something we will look at in more detail in the next chapter.

Chapter Summary

• Windows 10 is the upgrade of Windows 8.1, and is the most current version of Microsoft Windows operating system.

• Microsoft listened to the negative feedback that Windows 8.1 received, and have adapted Windows 10 to be more intuitive, more user-friendly, and full of lots of useful apps.

• It's the most powerful operating system Microsoft has ever produced – and the most complex. Yet it isn't hard to use; it's just a case of knowing what it can actually do, and how to find the different features.

Chapter 2: The Different Features Of Windows 10

This chapter will dig deeper into Windows 10 and explore its great features and new tricks that previous Windows versions don't have.

One of the most interesting features to start with is Continuum.

What Is Continuum?

This is a new feature for Windows. By knowing which device you're using at any given moment, Continuum can change the user interface to make it more appropriate to your screen, whether it's a PC, a 2 in 1 device, a phone, or a tablet.

Continuum was Microsoft's way of dealing with the negative feedback that came from Windows 8 in respect to having an interface that was totally touch-optimized – not great when you're using a desktop. Through Continuum, Windows can identify exactly what device you are using and then adapt the screen accordingly. In other words, Windows 10 has a device-optimized interface.

For example, if you are using a tablet, Windows will be able to detect that, and adjust the interface seamlessly for a touchscreen setup. Likewise, if you are using a traditional desktop, it will adapt the interface so it's most suitable for a mouse and keyboard. It even works on hybrid devices that combine both a desktop and touchscreen user experience by monitoring how you are using the device, and providing a tablet or desktop interface depending on whether its attached to the keyboard or not. It does this so quickly and effortlessly that your work won't be interrupted at all as it changes – you will simply switch from touchscreen to desktop with the same ease as if you were switching between two separate devices.

In addition to Windows switching the interface to suit the device, applications can also adapt to whichever platform you are using. Thanks to Universal Apps which all share the same coding, they can adapt to any device and interface without needing to open a new or separate version of the app.

When you're using a desktop, Windows 10 has the familiar layout that we all know and love from past Windows versions where the Start menu is in the left with all the shortcuts neatly organized. When you switch to a touchscreen, the layout will automatically change to Tablet Mode which is in the Windows 8 layout. You can continue working on your touchscreen device in this mode or you can opt out, either by reattaching your keyboard or changing to a desktop setup using the Tablet Mode icon at the bottom of the screen which asks you which mode you want to use.

The Start Menu

We've already talked about the start menu but let's look at it in more details as it's one of the features that we all use on Windows, and the one of the most complained about in Windows 8. The Start menu in Windows 10 has two columns – the first is a list in alphabetical order of all the shortcuts, and the other is all your apps neatly divided by 'Create', 'Explore', 'Games' and other categories, similar to the Windows 8 layout. You can switch these around and customize the way you want. The power button gives you the usual options of 'Shutdown', 'Hibernate', and 'Standby' and the search engine at the bottom allows you to search for programs, apps, files, and internet results, just like the older Windows 7. If you don't want to type every time you want to find an app, then you can pin your favorite apps to the Start menu, so you can access them easily.

Cortana

Cortana, exclusive to Windows 10, is the voice-controlled digital assistant that can make your life easier. Made for desktops, you can search for specific files and get quick answers to questions simply by asking your device, rather like Siri, or Google Now. Cortana can even send e-mails while you work on other tasks.

However, Cortana can do more than that. You can use this feature to mark events on your calendar, to set reminders, and set up relevant news stories.

To use Cortana, you need to set up voice recognition and make sure your region, speech, and language choices are set up to be consistent (for example, if your region is United Kingdom but your language choice is something different, Cortana won't be available. You can change this in the Settings option on the Start menu).

Xbox App

This is a new feature for Windows 10, and is great for anyone that loves the Xbox. It lets you play any Xbox One game on your desktop or tablet, and it also lets you record, edit, and share your game highlights. The Game DVR feature also continually records the last 30 seconds of the game, so any sudden wins won't be lost. You can also connect with friends on the games either through the usual Xbox platforms, or across Windows 10.

The New Internet Explorer – Microsoft Edge

The new internet explorer – known as Microsoft Edge – for Windows 10 is more than just a regular browser and has loads of new features that will allow you to interact with web pages in a totally new way. One especially handy trick is the note taking feature which lets you take notes on pages, highlight key pieces of information and either save the note later for future reference, or send to friends or colleagues. You can even share these notes through social media without ever leaving your browser. Other features include PDF support, a clever reading mode that reformats the layout of long or complex articles to make them easier to read and more user friendly, and – one of the most exciting features – is Cortana support, which helps you navigate through the sites. For example, on certain websites, Cortana will make suggestions in the address bar that are relevant to the content you're browsing. The great thing about Cortana's assistance is that it interacts with your browsing only when it's relevant – when the app wants to make a suggestion, you will see the Cortana icon moving so you can choose to click it and see the advice, or to ignore it. Here are some ways Cortana support on Microsoft Edge can be useful:

• Eating out: If you are browsing a restaurant's website, Cortana will pop up and provide you with relevant information such as the restaurant's address, phone number, directions, opening hours, reviews, menu, and distance from your location.

• Online purchases. If you regularly shop on retailer websites such as eBay or the Microsoft store, Cortana will pop up with discount codes related to your potential purchases.

• Music videos. You know those moments you are listening to your favorite song and you want to learn all the lyrics? Cortana can automatically bring up the lyrics of the song for you and list them down the side next to the music video. The app can also show you where you can purchase the song from.

• Sites with apps. If you are browsing a site with different apps, Cortana will show where you can download them from.

The Desktops And Split Screen

For maximum organization and ease, the new Multiple Desktops allows you to have several desktops which run separate windows - so it's like having multiple monitors but all on one screen. It's ideal for managing multiple programs, and organizing your desktops according to your tasks. For example, you can have one desktop for work with Word, PowerPoint, your e-mails, and internet explorer open. Then you can have another desktop just for a blog with Word and all your research tabs open on the internet. Finally, you can have a desktop where you leave

Amazon, your social media, and Netflix open. By clicking the 'Task View' at the bottom of the screen, you can switch through the different desktops with ease, and open new ones and close old ones with just a couple of clicks. If you are one of those people that likes to have everything divided into nice, neat compartments, this is for you.

Splitting the screen also got a whole lot easier and better. Although this feature isn't new, it's a better model, as previously you could only have a limited number of programs side-by-side depending on the screen resolution of your device. Now, you can split your screen in up to four different sections, letting you work on the different screens at the same time. For example, you can have Word open while keeping it side-by-side with internet explorer to have easy access to an article you are researching. To split the screen, simply drag the program to the corner of the desktop screen and it will divide into a quadrant. You can then drag the program's size to fill up half of the screen if you just want two programs side-by-side, or fill up the other quadrants with other programs by dragging them into the other corners.

Universal Apps

As we mentioned before, Universal Apps allow you to switch devices, and for the apps to follow suit and adjust with the change in interface. The apps all work the same way on whichever device you use, and will automatically carry over from one device to the next as they are stored on the OneDrive cloud, including Photos. Other apps that work in this way are Mail, Calendar, Video, Music, and People.

Office Apps

In Windows 10, the Office Apps are also touchscreen friendly and can be used on your phone or tablet with ease. Outlook also has a more finger-friendly user experience as e-mails can be deleted simply by swiping to the left. If you swipe to the right, you can mark the message as important as well as select other options.

Notification Area

After several versions of Windows without any central notification center, Microsoft has finally programmed one into Windows 10. For those who use iOS, Android, or other operating systems you'll probably already be familiar with this setup, yet it took a while for Windows to get on board. By clicking on the little speech bubble at the right-hand bottom of the screen, all your notifications will show up in one place. You can also access Settings there to make any updates or adjustments, as well as change the options for Airplane Mode, Network, and switch to Tablet Mode if you are on a desktop which has a touchscreen option.

The People App

Tucked into the right-hand corner of the task bar is the People app that allows you to connect easily and directly to the contacts in your e-mail and Skype lists. You can pin your favorite contacts in the list, so you can see all correspondence with them across multiple platforms, and contact them directly. It's a useful tool to separate contacts into groups such as family, friends, and work contacts, allowing you to interact with each group differently and easily send content to individuals or groups.

OneDrive

OneDrive did already exist, but now it's been upgraded and made even better. The potential of One Drive often gets overlooked, yet really, it's an amazing tool. Whatever files you have – Word documents, Excel spreadsheets, Photos, for example – you can easily save them to OneDrive which automatically saves them to the cloud, and then you can share view links of the file by default. In other words, this cloud saving system is automatically set up for you to use, and you don't need to save files or upload them using the account as it's already there on your computer. For example, if you are writing in a Word document and you want to save it, you can save it to OneDrive by clicking on the 'Save As' option. This means your documents are safe no matter what happens to your computer, as you can access them through your account on a different device if you need to. It also helps free up local storage space on your device.

These are the main key features that are unique to Windows 10 and make it the best version of Windows Microsoft has produced to date. The whole layout is designed to be intuitive and easy to use, whether you use it for regular, everyday use, or if you depend on your computer for work and need a system that helps you organize your different tasks. In a later chapter, we will look at how to use Windows 10, and how to access these apps and make them work for you. The next chapter though, will review some of the key benefits of Windows 10.

Chapter Summary

• There are several new or updated features that make Windows 10 superior to Windows 8 (although in the eyes of many users, that's not a hard feat) and other Windows versions.

• Some of its most exciting features include Continuum, which allows a smooth transition between different interfaces; Cortana, which acts as a digital assistant and can help streamline actions; and the Start menu, which has gone back to the good old column in the left side of the screen.

• Other improvements have been made to OneDrive, Office apps, multiple desktops, split screens, and Internet Explorer, now known as Microsoft Edge.

• Other interesting features include a central space for notifications, the People app, the Universal Apps, and the Xbox app.

Chapter 3: The Benefits Of Windows 10

If you have an older version of Windows and are not sure whether to upgrade to Windows 10 or not, this chapter is for you. Likewise, if you already have Windows 10 and you want to discover more about it, then you will find the following points helpful. This chapter looks at the key benefits of Windows 10.

• First, and perhaps the most important, Windows 10 offers a much better desktop and tablet experience than Windows 8. One of the major complaints against Windows 8 was that its looks were unappealing, it didn't function intuitively, and, at the end of the day, it just simply wasn't what customers wanted. Another problem was that key features were complex or hidden away, so that when it came to upgrading, many users were concerned that Windows 10 would be even more complex to navigate. Thankfully, Windows 10 isn't like that at all and it mixes the best aspects of the older Windows with some of the old parts of Windows 8, such as the desktop layout from older versions with the tablet layout from Windows 8 joined together in a much more logical, attractive way. If you are so put off with the 'tiles' layout from Windows 8 (that still exists in the touchscreen form), there is even an option to totally delete it. The most important part of the operating system – the interface – has now been made with the users' experiences and devices in mind, giving you a seamless experience and more control.

• Windows 10 is the best version of all the Microsoft Windows so far in terms of speed and features. It follows from Windows 8.1, which generally was disliked and considered an unwelcome upgrade by many Windows users.

• It has virtual desktops. Virtual desktops and multiple screens easily makes Windows 10 more superior. This may be a feature that is more exciting for those that use their computers for

14

several uses – such as entertainment purposes and for business – but those who fit in that category will love the simplicity and organization that multiple desktops bring.

• If you don't have Windows 10 yet and are taking the leap from Windows 7, then you are in for a treat – Windows 10 feels (and is) so much faster and more responsive than Windows 7. It also looks more modern and is laid out in a simple, logical way.

• Another great benefit for those moving from Windows 7 to Windows 10 is that Windows 10 is much safer and more secure thanks to Microsoft's Window Defender antivirus software, and the Windows Firewall. You don't even need to worry about installing any of this protection software as it's already enabled by default. Microsoft also added other software in addition to the two above that will protect against PC infections and malicious websites. There is also Windows Hello that allows biometric-based authentication, and is really easy to set up. Having your computer safer than ever is extremely reassuring, especially as hackers and viruses get increasingly crafty.

• You've probably used at some point, or at least heard of, Apple's Siri, and Google Now. Microsoft's version is Cortana, which can make your user experience a lot easier on your computer as you can rely on the app for reminders and alarms, to interact better with websites, plan trips, and to get the latest news. It's one of those apps where you don't know it's missing until you've used it and realized how much more convenient and easier it makes browsing and working on your computer.

• DirectX 12. If you don't play video games, then you can skip this point. However, if you use your computer to play PC games, then you will love this feature. It's only available on Windows 10 and Xbox One (as the Xbox play feature on Windows 10 lets you connect Xbox One and Windows 10) and it has Microsoft's new, powerful graphics technology. A lot of different games are using DirectX 12 for better quality graphics, high frame rates, and a much smoother experience; the difference is notable when compared to other graphic technology.

• More about games, the Xbox app brings the Xbox Live to your computer and lets you stream games from the Xbox One straight to your PC. This is great news for gamers. Another benefit of the Xbox app is that you can check your Xbox messages, see what your friends are up to, check out pre-recorded game clips, and keep up to date with game achievements.

These are the major benefits of using Windows 10, and they are significant enough to either make the move to Windows 10 or be happy that you have a great operating system if you already have it. The next chapter will look in more detail how to use Windows 10, so you can get the full benefits of all these new and upgraded features.

Chapter Summary

• Windows 10 is by far the most superior, powerful, and advanced version of Windows so far. It has some great new features that make an upgrade worthwhile.

• The main benefits include a more user-friendly and device-optimized interface; it has virtual desktops and multiple screens; it's much quicker and more modern than Windows 7; it has Cortana, a voice-activated digital assistant; it comes enabled with lots of different security and anti-virus software; visually, it's more attractive and appealing than Windows 8; and finally, it's made with gamers in mind who can enjoy better graphics and the compatibility between Xbox One and Windows 10.

Chapter 4: How To Use Windows 10

This chapter will guide you through using the different features and tricks in Windows 10.

How To Use Continuum

Continuum is already a part of Windows 10, so luckily you don't need to do much to set it all up. If you typically use a laptop or a desktop, then the operating system will be the same; the differences occur when you use tablets or hybrid devices as these will adjust to have a more touchscreen-friendly layout if you want.

When you take your tablet off the keyboard, a pop-up will appear asking if you want to enter Tablet Mode. Click on that, and you can select how you want the interface to look and it will be set up accordingly. When you put the tablet back on the keyboard stand, you will receive a pop-up asking what interface you want to use. You can control these prompts by setting an automatic response so Windows will automatically switch the interface to the way you want it, without sending you a prompt.

To do that, go to the Start Menu and click on 'Settings'. Then click 'System' and 'Tablet Mode'. There, you will see a heading that says 'When my device wants to switch modes' which takes you to a drop-down menu with three options:

• Never prompt me and always remain in current mode (select this and you basically turn off Continuum).

• Always prompt me to confirm (this keeps it in default mode).

• Never prompt me and always switch modes (this makes switching interfaces automatic).

Whatever you decide to choose, you can always change it at any time by following the steps above.

When your interface is in tablet mode you will notice, just like Windows 8, that the Start menu now takes the full screen. What's great about this new interface is that only some default tiles and the ones that you use the most (your pinned tiles), will appear large so you can easily access them. The others are small and kept neatly to the left-hand side.

If you are familiar with Windows 8, you will recall that you swiped from side to side to navigate through the Start page, but with Windows 10, you scroll up and down.

How To Use Cortana

To use Cortana, there are a couple of things you should know first. Cortana will access your personal information such as e-mails and documents, so if you feel uncomfortable sharing that much personal data with Microsoft, then it's best to make do without Cortana. However, if you're fine with that, then before you get started with Cortana's assistance, you need to adjust your privacy settings, especially in the Speech, Inking, and Typing section.

You need to turn on 'Getting to Know You' and 'Location'. 'Getting to Know You' allows Windows and Cortana to collect information such as contacts, your typing history, speech and handwriting patterns, and any recent calendar events. This helps make the experience more customized. If at any moment you decide you want to stop sharing data, you can switch this off (which means you also switch off Cortana), and the device will clear all the information it knows about you. 'Location' allows, as the name suggests, the app to see your location, and location history.

You can access Cortana from the search bar feature that's found to the left of the taskbar. Click in the search box and Cortana will open showing your interests, your calendar, and any questions you have asked. To the left-hand side of Cortana, you can click on the Notebook icon and configure Cortana the way you want, based around your preferences and hobbies, such as saving your favorite places or most used locations, and selecting different cards. Cards are like categories, such as Eat & Drink, Events,

Finance, News, and Movies & TV, among others, and can be switched on or off depending on what you want. They are related to your interests so, for example, Eat and Drink lets you receive different suggestions and recommendations from Foursquare that will be tailored to what you like.

If you click on the Lightbulb icon, you can set reminders which Cortana will organize by time and by people involved in the event.

One of the most exciting features of Cortana is that you can activate it using your voice. Starting with 'Hey Cortana', will prompt it to wait for your next command. This configuration goes even deeper as you can set Cortana so that it only responds to you, or you can allow it to respond to any voice. To get the voice activation working, you need to teach Cortana your voice. To do that, click 'Learn My Voice' and follow the next steps. You will have to read out loud six different statements that allows Cortana to recognize your voice. You can then make requests and ask Cortana questions.

Cortana can also be configured to detect tracking information in your e-mails – such as flights or packages – which will then be automatically stored as reminders or updates. You can choose to opt in or out of these services by changing the configurations in the Settings. There is also the option of 'Taskbar Tidbits' which allows Cortana to 'pipe up' (in the words of Windows) with some thoughts or greetings in the Search box. This may be an interesting novelty in the beginning, but you can also switch off this option too.

How To Sync Your iPhone With Windows 10

You don't need a MacBook to sync your iPhone to a computer – you can sync it with Windows 10 too. To sync them, connect your iPhone to your computer or your laptop and click 'Continue' when the pop-up requests access to your phone (you have to say 'Yes' here, otherwise you can't sync the device with the system).

Then, click the phone icon in the top bar and then click 'Sync' which should automatically sync the two devices. If that doesn't work, then you probably need to enable Sync. To do that, go to Music, Apps, Movies, TV Shows and Photos, and make sure the boxes are ticked that allow syncing. Then click 'Sync' again. If you have loads of data and files, this may be a slow process, so be prepared to wait a bit. Once that's done, check the folders on your phone to make sure all the data has gone from Windows 10 to your phone.

How To Use Microsoft Edge

Microsoft Edge is automatically set as the default browser and promises an easy, fast experience while navigating through the internet. As we have seen before though, it's more than just a browser and has a lot of really slick features.

First things first though, update the privacy settings on Edge. Open the browser and click the three little dots at the top right-hand corner and click 'Settings'. Then go down the list to 'View Advanced Settings'. From there, make sure the following three options are switched to 'On':

• Block pop-ups

• Send Do Not Track requests

• Block only third-party cookies

This keeps your browsing a little more private and protects your data.

Next, you can import your bookmarks from other internet browsers (Firefox, Chrome, and Internet Explorer) directly. If you have any issues – for example, sometimes Firefox doesn't always appear as an option – you can export them as a HTML file, then import them to Internet Explorer, and then finally import them to Microsoft Edge using Internet Explorer.

You will notice that Microsoft Edge is set to Bing search engine by default, which puts some people off of using it. However, you can switch to any other search engine so long as it supports the

OpenSearch standard. Google, for example, is supported. To update the search engine, go to the site of the search engine you want then click the three little dots at the top of the right-hand corner of the page. Scroll all the way down, then click 'Settings' and then click 'View Advanced Settings'. Then, click the Bing menu and select the engine you want instead (for example, if you searched Google in the browser, it will automatically provide that as an option). Then click 'Add as Default'.

Cortana is automatically enabled into your Microsoft Edge and, as we saw, it can provide various suggestions and recommendations based on what you are looking for and the pages you are reading. This can be a useful feature, but if it's not something you want, then you can switch it off. To do so, click the three dots in the upper right-hand corner and go to 'Settings'. From there, click 'View Advanced Settings' and scroll down until you find 'Get Cortana to Assist me in Microsoft Edge'. Then, switch that to 'Off'.

You can also adjust how you read text by going to the three dots in the corner, going to 'Settings', and then to 'Reading'. Click and open the 'Reading View Style'. There, you can choose different background colors – light, medium, and dark or white, gray, and black – and different font sizes too!

Like other browsers, you can create a reading list by using the star button in the main toolbar to save articles that you may want to read later. To see your reading lists, go to the shooting star symbol up the top, and click on what looks like a pile of books (that's your Reading List). There you can see all your bookmarked articles. Once you've read them and want to remove them, just right click on the link and click 'Remove'.

One feature we've already discussed is that you can make notes on web pages and share with others. To do this, click on the three dots at the top and click 'Add Notes'. This will freeze the page and let you highlight it, add text, make drawings, or mark anything on that webpage. Once you're finished, you can then either save the note to OneNote, download it onto your desktop, add it to your Favorites, or save it to your Reading List. You can even share it with other people by clicking 'Share' and sending it through Facebook or Twitter. However, these social media apps are not set by default, and you will need to install them separately.

How To Customize The Start Menu

One of the most exciting things about Windows 10 is just how flexible and open it is to customization.

To change the size of the Start menu, open the Start menu and move your cursor arrow to the top of the menu. When the cursor is resting on the edge, it should turn into the shape of a double-edged arrow. You can then move it up and down until you reach the size you like. That size will be automatically set until you change it again.

You can also make the Start menu into a full screen, so you can easily see all the different apps and icons. To do this, go to the Start menu and click 'Settings'. Then click on 'Personalization' and then 'Start'. Then enable 'Use Start Full Screen' by turning it on. Any time you click 'Start' from now on, it will go into full-screen mode. To change it back, just follow the steps above and switch it off.

If there is an app you use a lot or want easy access to, you can pin it from any location on your computer to your Start menu. For example, if you want an app on your desktop to be added to the Start menu, right click on the app and click 'Pin to Start'. That's it – it will then be added to your Start menu. If you want to unpin it from the Start menu, right click the app and click 'Unpin from Start', and it will be returned to its original place.

In the Start menu, you have different tiles for different apps and categories. This is mostly for aesthetics, but you can resize the tiles by right clicking on any of the apps in the Start menu and clicking 'Resize'. You can choose between small, medium, wide, or large. You can also move tiles around the Start menu by dragging the tile to the place you want and then letting go. It will automatically fall into the place you drag it to.

The Start menu in Windows 10 is set to a default color which you can change and customize to your preference. To do that, you just need to click on the Start menu and click 'Settings'. Then click 'Personalization', and then 'Colors'. You can then choose the color you want.

How To Use The Xbox App

The Xbox App can be used to record gameplay. However, you can record pretty much any running app, whether it's a game or not. In other words, you can use it to record games and to capture screen actions.

To do this, you first need to log into the Xbox App, and then you can start recording a game or an app. To do this, press the Windows button (on your keyboard) and G at the same time to open the Game Bar. A box will ask you if the app is a game, and you just need to click the box next to the option, 'Yes, this is a game'. Then click on the little red circle to start recording, and when you want to finish recording, press the Windows button and the 'G' at the same time, and then click the red circle again to finish recording.

Tip: If you have already told the app that you are a recording a game, then you can use a nifty shortcut to start and stop recording. You just need to press Windows, Alt, and R at the same time. To access your clips, just go to the Action Center (you can access this by simultaneously pressing the Windows button and 'A') and your clips will be saved there. Not all apps can be recorded – Skype for the desktop, for example, can't be – but most apps you can record.

You can record the last 30 seconds of any game using the 'Record That' feature. This is useful for those moments when you do something incredible and you want to keep that moment as a reminder or to show someone else later. It records your game constantly when you're playing and keeps just the previous 30 seconds. You can change the time it records – the 30 seconds is simply there by default – from a minimum of 15 seconds to a maximum of 10 minutes. Once a section of the game is recorded, it will be saved, and you can edit it later. To get this feature working, open the Xbox App and click on 'Settings'. Click the 'Game DVR' icon and switch on the 'Record

That' feature. You'll see next to it, that you can adjust the times using the 'Record the Last' option. Once you've set that up, go to the game you want to record, press Windows and 'G' together, which will open the Game Bar, and select 'Yes, this is a Game'. The next time you play a game, you just need to open the Game Bar and click to access 'Record That'.

How To Stream Xbox Games To Your Computer

If you always play your Xbox One on a shared TV and someone wants to watch a film, this feature will save you the disappointment of not being able to finish your game. It allows you to stream your Xbox games straight to your computer. To do this, go to your Xbox One and open 'Settings', click 'Preferences', and activate 'Allow Game Streaming to Other Devices'. Then, go back to your computer and confirm that both your PC and Xbox are using the same network. Open the Xbox app, click 'Connect' in the left-hand side, and select your PC from the list of apps available. Then, click 'Xbox', and when it connects, click 'Stream'. From there, it's easy. Just go to your Xbox, click 'My Games', and click 'Play From Console' on whichever game you want to play.

How To Use The People App

As we saw before, the People app on Windows 10 is a great tool for managing contacts. It works as both an address book, and as a single app where you can store all your Skype and Outlook contacts. It also allows you to see all the messages you have exchanged with a person across the Skype and Outlook channels. It also links to your calendar, so you will receive reminders of birthdays and other significant events or dates.

To add contacts, open the People app from your Start menu, and go to Settings. Click 'Add Account' and you can select an account – such as a Gmail account – to import the contacts from. If there are contacts you want to add manually, just click the plus sign in Contacts, and fill out as much information as possible.

A useful tool in the People app is that you can choose which contacts you see and which ones you keep hidden. The default is set to show all contacts, but if you want to change that, go to Settings, click on 'Filter Contact List', and then choose the platforms from where you want to see the contacts.

How To Split Your Screen

This is an incredibly useful app if you are working from multiple apps, as Windows 10 allows you to split your screen up to four times. Once you've split your screen, you will still be able to open other apps – such as your browser – and they will appear full-screen without affecting your split screen.

It's simple to split your screen – just get the app, page, or document you want to split, drag it to the left or right, bottom or top corner of your PC screen and it will automatically fill a quadrant. You can then stretch it to fill half of the screen if you want. Repeat up to four times with other apps.

How To Use Multiple Desktops

In theory, you can add an unlimited number of desktops to your PC using this tool. To add a virtual desktop, just open the 'Task View' at the bottom corner on the left-hand side in the task bar (it's next to the Search option), or by pressing the Windows key and the Tab button together. You will see that you can view all the pages you have open in one go, and at the bottom of the page in the right-hand corner, there will be an option to 'Add New Desktop'. You can switch between desktops by opening the tab panel and selecting the desktop you want to work from.

You can move pages and windows to other desktops too. Open the 'Task View' and right click on the page you want to move. Then select 'Move To' and choose the desktop you want it to be in.

To close a desktop, just open the 'Task View' and hover the cursor over the desktop you want to close. A red box with a white X will appear in the corner. Just click on that, and it will close the desktop.

These are some of the main features in Windows 10. They are easy to use once you know the basic instructions, and by now you should be able to start making the most of the operating system's new and upgraded apps. The next chapter will answer the most frequently asked questions regarding Windows 10.

Chapter Summary

• This chapter showed you how to use the following: Continuum, Cortana, Microsoft Edge, the Start menu, the Xbox App, how to stream Xbox games onto your computer, the People app, split screens, using multiple desktops, and how to sync your iPhone to Windows 10.

Chapter 5: Frequently Asked Questions

In this chapter, you will find all the answers to the most frequently asked questions about Windows 10.

How much does Windows 10 cost?

The prices vary, but for Windows 10 Home, it will cost about $120, and for Windows 10 Pro (which is more for business and professional use) it costs around $200.

Can my computer support Windows 10?

If you are currently using Windows 8.1 or Windows 7 and your computer has all the system requirements – 1GHZ processor; RAM 1GB for 32-bit or 2GB for 64-bit; 16GB for 32-bit OS, 20GB for 64-bit OS; DirectX 9 graphics card; display of 800x600 – you can upgrade to Windows 10 directly. If you buy a new PC, it's likely that Windows 10 is already installed.

For older versions of Windows – Windows XP or Windows Vista for example – it's likely your computer won't support Windows 10. If you really want Windows 10 and want to get a new computer anyway, it's better to purchase a new PC with Windows 10 pre-installed.

I want to upgrade to Windows 10, but I have apps on my computer that I want to keep. Will they still be there?

An upgrade is not that intrusive and doesn't remove apps you have installed on Windows 7 or 8. After upgrading to Windows 10, all your apps will still be there – plus some new ones!

In terms of compatibility, if you're upgrading from Windows 7 or 8, it's probable that most apps will be absolutely fine and work on Windows 10. Apps on older versions of Windows though, may not function on Windows 10.

How many editions exist of Windows 10?

There are a lot – currently, there are 12 different editions, and upgrades and tweaks happen regularly. These are made with different audiences in mind, such as business consumers, and families. The main two you will probably see are:

• Windows 10 Home: This is the most common for the everyday user and for small businesses. It's the cheapest edition and you still get all the main features.

• Windows 10 Pro: This covers a few extra features such as a remote desktop server, and Hyper-V virtualization, and is most popular among businesses, IT professionals, and Windows fans.

How do I know which Windows I'm on now?

To find out which version of Windows you currently have, go to the Start menu, click 'Settings', then open 'System', and click 'About'. There you will see all the information related to your PC, including which edition of Windows it's running on.

My Cortana isn't working. Why?

There are a few reasons why your Cortana may not be working. First, you may need to adjust your privacy settings, as Cortana needs permission to access the 'Getting to Know You' app, and your 'Location' app. If that is all in order, then check the 'Notebook' icon as that may not be enabled, due to the fact that Cortana isn't enabled. To check that, go to Cortana, go to Settings, and make sure that you turn on 'Cortana Can Give You Suggestions, Ideas, Reminders, Alerts'.

If that's all fine and your Cortana is working but not the voice activation, check your microphone and your speakers.

Sometimes if the microphone has been disabled, Cortana won't be able to hear your commands and function properly.

Finally, it could be that Cortana isn't supported in your country, or it could be that your country, language, and speech language are not aligned.

If it's the latter, then you need to adjust the settings so that everything is aligned. For example, if the operating system settings are adjusted so that the country is set to the United States, but Windows display language is set to English (United Kingdom), it won't work.

If you are in Australia, you need to make sure your country is set to Australia, the language is set to English (Australian), and the speech language is set to English (Australian). Likewise, if you are in Japan, the language must be set to Japanese, and the speech language to Japanese, if you are in Italy, the country must be set to Italy, the language set to Italian, and the speech language set to Italian, and so on.

To do this, go to Settings in the Start menu and select 'Time and Language' and then select 'Region and Language'. Check what language is set for the Windows display language and select your desired language, then click 'Add Language'. Then update the location and download the language pack, if needs be, under 'Speech'. Once that's done, go back to 'Time and Language' and set your new language to 'Set as Default'.

Once everything is aligned, wait a few minutes before checking to see if Cortana is available. If after five minutes it still isn't there, try signing out of your account and signing back in. If that still doesn't work, then try restarting the computer. That should be enough to get Cortana fully enabled.

Some webpages don't open on Microsoft Edge. Why?

Microsoft Edge supports just one plugin which is Adobe Flash. This means that some websites, those supported by other plugins, either may not function properly, or not open at all. If that's the case, then just go to the three dots in the right-hand corner of the top of the page and choose the 'Open with Internet Explorer' option. That should open the webpage properly.

If you want to avoid having this issue again, you can set Internet Explorer as your default browser. To do this, go to the Start menu and click 'Settings'. From there, open 'System' and click 'Default Apps'. Go down the list until you come to 'Web Browser'. Then click 'Microsoft Edge' and choose your desired installed browser.

Is my personal data safe on Windows 10?

Windows 10, like any other operating system, does collect some personal information. For example, if your system crashes or it fails to diagnose specific issues, Windows will gather these reports and it will also track information based on what apps you use, how you interact with them, and for how long. The information gathered about how you use your apps has troubled some people and there is a way of preventing it. To stop Microsoft from collecting your app usage data, go to Settings in the Start menu, click 'Feedback and Diagnostics', and where you see 'Diagnostic and Usage Data', select 'Basic'. This stops information about your apps being sent to Microsoft.

Cortana also has access to your e-mails and other personal data which is necessary to give you a fully-functional and personalized experience. It also has access to your location. If you deny this access, Cortana won't work.

According to Microsoft, it doesn't gather your personal information beyond what is listed in the privacy statement. There isn't any evidence to suggest that Microsoft has breached these terms, nor that it is secretly checking your files.

I upgraded my Windows version to Windows 10, but now I have less storage than before. Why?

If you have upgraded from Windows 7 or Windows 8 to Windows 10 and you find your PC suddenly has less storage than before, there is a good reason for that (and luckily it can be fixed). It's because after you upgrade, your old Windows is still on your PC saved as 'windows.old' and doesn't just disappear. You can't see it but it's there, hanging around, taking up valuable space.

The reason why Microsoft keeps the old files on your PC is to give you the choice to go back to the older version if you wish to. However, if you really love your new Windows 10, then you can delete the old one and this will give you a lot more space on your PC. In the search area next to the Start menu, type 'cleanup' and click on 'Disk Cleanup'. Click the main drive where your operating system is stored. Then click the option to delete the previous windows installations.

My Windows 10 does updates at the most inconvenient times without telling me. How do I stop this?

Automatic updates are a pain, especially if you're in the middle of working on something and suddenly everything shuts down and you're treated to a blank screen, telling you how much percent of updates are done. However, there is a way of stopping this. Head to the Start menu and go to Settings. From there, open 'Update' and 'Security' then click 'Advanced Options'. Then change the 'Notify' settings to 'Schedule Restart', which means Windows will ask you when you would like to do the updates rather than just doing them at random and with no warning.

How can I watch DVDs on my Windows 10 PC?

The standard option for Windows 10 comes without DVD playing software, and to get the app known as Windows DVD Player, you must download it from the Windows Store which costs around $15.

There is another way of watching DVDs though and that's through VLC Media Player. It supports Windows 10 and is free to download.

I want to set up Windows Hello but it's not working. Why?

By setting up Windows Hello, you can log into your PC using face recognition or fingerprint. To use it though, you must have a computer that has the necessary hardware – unfortunately, older computers just won't be able to support it.

To set it up, go to Account in the Start menu and select 'Change Account Settings'. You will then need to select 'Sign-in Options' and create a pin. From there, simply follow the step-by-step instructions.

My Windows 10 is using so much data. Why, how do I stop it?

This may be an issue if you are using a tablet with 4G, using a smartphone with Windows 10, or using a mobile hotspot. Why is there an issue? Windows 10 uses a lot of data when it's left in the default setting, which can quite quickly take you over your data allowance – and present you with an unpleasant bill at the end of the month.

The way to stop this is to change the configurations. Go to Settings in the Start menu and click on 'Network and Internet'. Then select 'Wi-Fi' and go to 'Advanced Options'. Switch to 'Set as Metered Connection', which will stop Windows from using so much data.

My apps had no problems on Windows 8.1 but suddenly when I open them on Windows 10, some of them are blurry. Why?

Sometimes, Windows 10 has compatibility issues with high-resolution displays which causes some apps – that were previously working fine – to suddenly become blurry. There are two ways to fix this. First, go to the Control Panel (search for it in the Start menu and it will come up) and go to Display. From there on, there is no set standard to fix the blurriness; you just need to play around with the options and settings there until you find what fixes the blurry view the best.

The other way is to go directly to the app that has the problem, and right click on it. Click on 'Properties' and then open the 'Compatibility' option. Tick the 'Disable Display Scaling on High DPI Settings', which should do the trick.

These are the answers to some of the most commonly asked questions when it comes to Windows 10. The operating system is logical and once you get the hang of adjusting the settings of a couple of apps, you'll see how the same procedures are equal across the board. Windows 10 is an excellent system – as mentioned before, Microsoft's best to date – yet it still has a couple of hiccups now and again, the main ones of which we covered here.

Conclusion

Congratulations! You've reached the end of the book and now should be ready to dive head-first into using the Windows 10 operating system!

By now, you should have a much better idea of the kind of professional and high-tech tool that your PC has. Instead of just being a system that is there to support your internet browsing and Office app uses, Windows 10 can be such a useful tool, no matter what your interests are.

Whether you are a professional that uses the computer daily for work or someone that simply likes to browse now and again online, there should be at least one new feature that you can now use that will make your user experience more efficient and more effective.

I hope this book has helped you realize that understanding operating systems on your computer is not just for IT professionals, nor for Windows enthusiasts – it can be for anyone. The amount of technology we have at our fingertips without even realizing it is truly astonishing.

Thank you for choosing this book, and I hope you enjoy exploring how broad and deep the technology in Windows 10 runs. Happy browsing!

www.ingramcontent.com/pod-product-compliance
Lightning Source LLC
Chambersburg PA
CBHW060935050326
40689CB00013B/3102